Volcanoes!

Anne Schreiber

NATIONAL GEOGRAPHIC
Washington, D.C.

For Harrison
—A.S.

Published by the National Geographic Society, Washington, D.C. 20036.

Library of Congress Cataloging-in-Publication Data

Schreiber, Anne.
Volcanoes! / by Anne Schreiber.
p. cm. -- (National geographic readers series)
ISBN 978-1-4263-0285-5 (trade paper : alk. paper) -- ISBN 978-1-4263-0287-9
(library : alk. paper)
1. Volcanoes -- Juvenile literature. I. Title.
QE521.3.S34 2008
551.21--dc22
2007049743

Printed in the United States of America

Front Cover, 24 (top), 32 (top, right): © Digital Vision; 1: © Robert Glusic/Digital Vision/Getty Images; 2: © Shutterstock; 4-5: © Bruce Davidson/npl/Minden Pictures; 6, 32 (center, left): © Stuart Armstrong; 7, 32 (bottom, right): © Bryan Lowry/SeaPics.com; 8-9: © Yann Arthus-Bertrand/CORBIS; 9 (inset), 12-13: © Martin S. Walz; 10: © Doug Perrine/SeaPics.com; 11: © Pierre Vauthey/CORBIS SYGMA; 14 (top): © WEDA/epa/CORBIS; 14 (bottom): © Goodshoot/CORBIS; 15 (top): Mike Doukas and Julie Griswold/USGS; 15 (bottom), 32 (bottom, right): © Pete Oxford/Minden Pictures/Getty Images; 16 (inset), 27 (top): JPL/NASA; 16-17: © Phil Degginger/Mira.com/drr.net; 18-19: K. Segerstrom/USGS; 20-21: © Francesco Ruggeri/Getty Images; 22 (inset), 32 (top, left): Cyrus Read/AVO/USGS; 22-23: Gateway to Astronaut Photography of the Earth/JSC/NASA; 24 (bottom): © J.D. Griggs/CORBIS; 25 (top): © CORBIS; 25 (bottom): © Rebecca Freeman/Tulane University; 26: © John Stanmeyer/VII; 27 (center): © H. Poitrenaud/AFP/Getty Images; 27 (bottom): © Art Wolfe/The Image Bank/Getty Images; 28: © John Cornforth/SeaPics.com; 29 (top): © John Harvey Photos: 29 (center): © Joseph Van Os/The Image Bank/Getty Images; 29 (bottom): © Bo Zaunders/CORBIS; 30-31: © Norbert Rosing/National Geographic Image Collection, 32 (center, right): © Jeremy Horner/CORBIS.

Table of Contents

Mountains of Fire!

Ash and steam pour out of the mountain. Hot melted rock rises up inside the mountain. Suddenly a spray of glowing hot ash shoots out. It is an eruption!

More melted rock is forced out. It spills down the side of the volcano in a burning hot river. Anything that cannot move is burned or buried.

KIMANURA VOLCANO
ZAIRE

WORD BLAST

ERUPTION: When magma reaches Earth's surface. Some eruptions are explosive.

Hot Rocks

When magma comes
out of the Earth it is
called lava.
The lava hardens.
Ash and rock pile up.
A volcano is born.

ASH

VENT

LAVA

MAGMA
CHAMBER

Deep beneath the Earth's surface it is hot. Hot enough to melt rock. When rock melts it becomes a thick liquid called magma. Sometimes it puddles together in a magma chamber. Sometimes it finds cracks to travel through. If magma travels through a crack to the surface, the place it comes out is called a vent.

WORD BLAST

MAGMA: Thick, liquid melted rock.
MAGMA CHAMBER: A space deep underground filled with melted rock.
VENT: Any opening in Earth's surface where volcanic materials come out.

Shaky Plates

Where do cracks and vents
in the Earth come from?

The land we live on is broken into pieces
called plates. The plates fit Earth like a
puzzle. They are always moving a few
inches a year. When plates pull apart...
or smash together...watch out!

This picture shows the gap that forms when plates pull apart.

THINGVELLIR, ICELAND

NORTH AMERICA

EUROPE

Atlantic Ocean

AFRICA

SOUTH AMERICA

Pacific Ocean

— Earth's Plates

Mid-Atlantic Ridge

One place where Earth's plates smash together is called the Mid–Atlantic Ridge. It is the longest mountain range on Earth and most of it is underwater.

9

An Island Is Born

What happens when two plates pull apart?
They make a giant crack in the Earth.
Magma can rise up through these cracks.
This even happens underwater.

About 60 million years ago an underwater volcano poured out so much lava, it made new land. A huge island grew, right in the middle of the ocean. Lava formed the country of Iceland!

SURTSEY

About 50 years ago, people saw smoke coming out of the ocean near Iceland. A new island was being born right before their eyes! They called it Surtsey, after the Norse god of fire.

The Ring of Fire

Karymsky
Volcano

ASIA

Pacific Ocean

Indian Ocean

Mount
Merapi

Ring of Fire
Earth's plates
Mountains
Active volcanoes

AUSTRALIA

What happens when plates bump into
each other? Maybe a mountain will be
pushed a little higher. Maybe a volcano
will erupt. There may be an earthquake,
or a tsunami, or both!

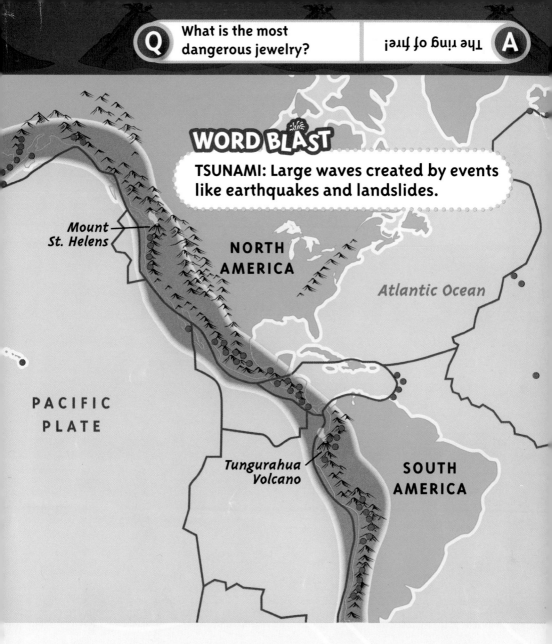

WORD BLAST

TSUNAMI: Large waves created by events like earthquakes and landslides.

Mount St. Helens

NORTH AMERICA

Atlantic Ocean

PACIFIC PLATE

Tungurahua Volcano

SOUTH AMERICA

The edge of the Pacific plate is grinding into the plates around it. The area is called the Ring of Fire. Many of Earth's earthquakes and volcanoes happen in the Ring of Fire.

Postcards from the Ring

I Lava You!

Mount Merapi, Indonesia

Moose You Very Much!

Karymsky Volcano, Kamchatka

Washing You A Great Day!

From the Cascade Mountains in Washington State

Mount St. Helens

HAVING A HOT TIME IN THE ANDES!

Tungurahua Volcano, Ecuador

Meet a Volcano... Or Three

Not all volcanoes are the same. What kind they are depends on how they erupt.

The lava from a shield volcano is hot and liquid. Rivers of lava flow from the volcano's vents. These lava flows create a gently sloping volcano.

HOT FACT

Olympus Mons on Mars is a shield volcano. It is the largest volcano in our solar system! Seen from above, it is round, like a shield.

MAUNA LOA

The Hawaiian myth of Pele tells the story of how Pele, goddess of earth and fire, built a home on Mauna Loa. Violent volcanic eruptions are said to be Pele losing her temper.

Meet Mauna Loa!

PARICUTIN VOLCANO

A cone volcano has straight sides and tall, steep slopes. These volcanoes have beautiful eruptions. Hot ash and rocks shoot high into the air. Lava flows from the cone.

One day a cone volcano started erupting in a field in Mexico. It erupted for nine years. When it stopped it was almost as high as the Empire State Building.

Even though Paricutin stopped exploding in 1952, the ground around it is still hot! Scientists guess that Paricutin spit out 10 trillion pounds of ash and rock.

A stratovolcano is like a layer cake.
First, lava shoots out and coats the
mountain. Then come rock and ash.
Then, more lava. The mountain builds
up with layers of lava, rock, and ash.

Meet Mount Etna!

MOUNT ETNA, ITALY

There is a myth about Vulcan, a Roman god of fire and iron. He lived under Vulcan Island, near Mount Etna. Every time Vulcan pounded his hammer, a volcano erupted. The word *volcano* comes from the name Vulcan.

The True Story Of Crater Lake

Crater Lake may seem like a regular lake, but it is actually a stratovolcano. It was once a mountain called Mount Mazama. Now it is a deep, clear lake in Oregon.

An explosion over 6,000 years ago blew the top off Mount Mazama. Lava, dust, and ash swept down the mountain. The mountaintop fell in and a giant caldera was formed. Over time the caldera, a crater, filled with water. It is the deepest lake in the United States.

WORD BLAST

CALDERA: A caldera is formed when the top of a volcano caves in.

CRATER LAKE

After the mountain collapsed, there were more eruptions. In one, a small cinder cone of ash and lava was formed. This cinder cone pokes out of the lake. It is called Wizard Island.

Volcanoes Rock!

PAHOEHOE

NAME: Pahoehoe (say Pa-hoy-hoy)

HOW IT FORMS: Fast, hot, liquid lava hardens into smooth rope-like rock.

SPECIAL POWER: It hardens into beautiful and weird shapes known as Lava Sculptures.

AA

NAME: Aa (say Ah-ah)

HOW IT FORMS: The crust on top of Aa lava hardens into sharp mounds of rocks.

SPECIAL POWER: It can cut right through the bottom of your shoes!

PELE'S HAIR

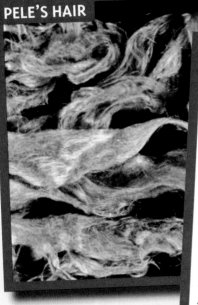

NAME: Pele's Hair (say Pel-lay)

HOW IT FORMS: Lava fountains throw lava into the air where small bits stretch out and form glass threads.

SPECIAL POWER: These strands of volcanic glass are super thin and long, just like hair! Small tear-shaped pieces of glass, called Pele's tears, sometimes form at the end of Pele's Hair.

PUMICE

NAME: Pumice (say Puh-miss)

HOW IT FORMS: In a big explosion, molten rock can get filled with gas from the volcano. When the lava hardens the gas is trapped inside.

SPECIAL POWER: The gas makes the rock so light, it can float on water.

Volcanic
Record Breakers

Indonesia, a string of islands in the Ring of Fire, has **more erupting volcanoes** than anywhere else on Earth.

JAVA ISLAND

The place with the **most volcanic activity** is not on Earth. It is on Io, one of Jupiter's moons!

The 1883 explosion of Krakatau was the **loudest sound** in recorded time. People heard the explosion over 2,500 miles away. Anak Krakatau, which means "Child of Krakatau," is a volcano that was born in 1927 where Krakatau used to be.

Mount Etna is the **largest active volcano** in Europe.

Hot Spots

Do you want to visit somewhere really hot? Check out these hot spots—places on Earth where magma finds its way through the Earth's crust. Hot spots are heated by volcanic activity!

The Hawaiian Islands are all volcanic mountains. They start on the sea floor and poke out above the sea. Kilauea in Hawai'i is still erupting. As long as it keeps erupting the island of Hawai'i keeps growing.

On Kyushu Island, in Japan, some people use the hot springs to boil their eggs.

Take a bath with the monkeys in Japan.

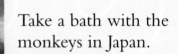

In Iceland, you can swim in pools heated by volcanoes.

Exploding Ending

If you visit Yellowstone National Park, you will be standing on one of the biggest supervolcanoes on Earth. Yellowstone sits on an ancient caldera. Magma still bubbles and boils a few miles below ground.

Yellowstone has a lot of geysers—more than 300. The magma below Yellowstone caldera heats underground water. The water boils and bursts to the surface as geysers, spraying steam and hot water high into the air.

Go to Yellowstone and see Earth in action!

CALDERA
A caldera is formed when the top of a volcano caves in.

MAGMA
Thick, liquid melted rock.

MAGMA CHAMBER
A space deep underground filled with melted rock.

TSUNAMI
Large waves created by events like earthquakes and landslides.

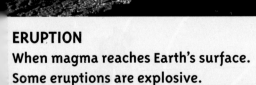

ERUPTION
When magma reaches Earth's surface. Some eruptions are explosive.

VENT
Any opening in Earth's surface where volcanic materials come out.